NEW VANGUARD • 183

WARSHIPS OF THE ANGLO-DUTCH WARS 1652–74

ANGUS KONSTAM   ILLUSTRATED BY PETER BULL

First published in Great Britain in 2011 by Osprey Publishing,
Midland House, West Way, Botley, Oxford, OX2 0PH, UK
44–02 23rd St, Suite 219, Long Island City, NY 11101, USA
E-mail: info@ospreypublishing.com

Osprey Publishing is part of the Osprey Group

A CIP catalogue record for this book is available from the British Library

Print ISBN: 978 1 84908 410 9
PDF e-book ISBN: 978 1 84908 411 6
EPUB e-book ISBN: 978 1 84908 889 3

Page layout by Melissa Orrom Swan, Oxford
Index by Michael Parkin
Typeset in Sabon and Myriad Pro
Originated by Blenheim Colour Ltd
Printed in China through Worldprint Ltd

11 12 13 14 15   10 9 8 7 6 5 4 3 2 1

Osprey Publishing is supporting the Woodland Trust, the UK's leading
woodland conservation charity by funding the dedication of trees.

www.ospreypublishing.com

CONTENTS

WARSHIPS OF THE ANGLO-DUTCH WARS 1652–74

INTRODUCTION

On 30 January 1649, with a single stroke of an axe, England became a republic. The execution of King Charles I marked a turning point in British history. It drew a line under the turmoil of the preceding years of Civil War, and established Parliament as the sole authority in the land. Within months the fledgling republic would ratify its existence and become a Commonwealth, encompassing the three kingdoms of England, Ireland and Scotland, all

This dramatic painting of the HMS *Resolution* in a gale by Willem van de Velde the Younger captures all the elegance of warships of this period. The 70-gun Third Rate was launched in Harwich in 1667, under the supervision of Anthony Deane. (NMM BHC3582).

of which had been ruled by the late king. While another Civil War would follow before Scotland and Ireland were fully brought into line, this new Commonwealth was also able to look beyond Britain's shores, as it sought to rebuild England's battered economy through maritime trade, and to regain her standing as a European power.

Meanwhile, on the far side of the North Sea the Dutch Republic had become the leading mercantile power in Europe. The Dutch defeat of the Spanish at the battle of the Downs in 1639 freed the republic from the threat of by their former overlords, and removed the risk posed by the Spanish fleet on Dutch maritime trade. While the rest of Europe was being dragged through the horrors of the Thirty Years War (1618–48), the Dutch seized the opportunity to develop their global trade routes, and to establish control of the East Indies. This was achieved at the expense of Portugal – then a vassal state of Spain – and it also prevented other European interlopers – most notably England – from gaining control of the same lucrative archipelago. While on land they offered military support to their Protestant allies, they also built up a powerful navy. It was this fleet that wrested control of the seas from the Spaniards, and which, by 1649, had become the dominant naval force in Europe.

The Commonwealth realized that the Dutch posed a latent threat to the expansion of maritime trade, and consequently they set about enlarging the 'State's Fleet'. While the Dutch firmly controlled the Spice Islands of the East Indies, English merchants – most notably the East India Company – were able to establish a trading presence on the coast of India, and so gain their own small share of the spice trade. After the horrors of the Civil War, English merchants were eager to re-establish their trading links on the far side of the Indian Ocean, as well as in the nascent English colonies in North America.

As Anglo-Dutch mercantile rivalry increased, so too did the tension between the two navies, who patrolled the same north European waters, and who warily gauged the growing power of their rivals.

Ostensibly, the First Anglo-Dutch War (1652–54) erupted over the issue of 'sovereignty of the seas', or rather claims over the establishment of territorial waters. This was little more than the catalyst. The war was really fought over maritime trade – the control and protection of trade routes – and to establish naval and therefore economic dominance over their opponents. The war really didn't achieve these aims, and so the Second Anglo-Dutch War (1665–67) and the Third Anglo-Dutch

General-at-Sea Robert Blake (1598–1657) was the most gifted naval commander of either side during the three Anglo-Dutch Wars. In the first conflict he steered the Commonwealth fleet to victory, an achievement that justly earned him the title of 'father of British seapower'. Painting by an unknown English artist (NMM BHC2559).

War (1672–74) were really about unfinished business – fought to resolve the issue of naval mastery once and for all. What is particularly notable about these three conflicts is that, apart from the odd raid, these campaigns were fought exclusively at sea. The result was a series of brief but titanic struggles between rival battle fleets of sailing warships – the first conflict of its kind in history.

This small book tells the story of these rival fleets, of the ships that composed them, and of the crews who forged a new chapter in naval history by developing a new kind of warfare. The size of this book means that this can never be more than a primer – a small taster of the subject. By necessity it also concentrates more on the English fleet that the Dutch, largely because information on its ships is more readily available. However, the aim is to present a balanced view, and to show how the sailing warship of both nations developed during this period, and how both English and Dutch admirals rewrote the book on naval warfare. If it goes even some way to shedding light on these stirring times, then it has achieved its purpose.

The reign of King Charles II of England and Scotland (reigned 1660–85) brought to an end England's experiment with Republican government. While foreign relations were dominated by the Anglo-Dutch wars, Charles's reign is more generally associated with royal hedonism, courtly excess, the Great Plague and the Great Fire of London (Walker Art Gallery, Liverpool).

CHRONOLOGY

1649	January	Execution of King Charles I
	February	Mutiny in Parliamentarian fleet
		Rank of General-at-Sea established
1650	November	Destruction of Royalist fleet in Mediterranean

1652–54 First Anglo-Dutch War

1652	19 May	First clash off Dover.
	7 June	Declaration of War
	28 September	Battle of Kentish Knock – English victory
	28 November	Battle of Dungeness – Dutch victory
1653	18–20 February	Battle of Portland – English victory
	4 March	Battle of Leghorn (Livorno) – Dutch victory
	20 March	English issue '*Fighting Instructions*'
	April	Rump Parliament overthrown – Cromwell becomes Lord Protector
	2 June	Battle of the Gabbard – English victory
	31 July	Battle of Scheveningen – English victory
1654	September	Treaty of Westminster – peace
	November	Commonwealth declares war with Spain
1655	May	English capture Jamaica from the Spanish
1657	23 April	Battle of Santa Cruz – English victory
1658	3 September	Death of Lord Protector
1660	May	Restoration of King Charles II as King of England and Scotland

1665–67 Second Anglo-Dutch War

| 1665 | March | Declaration of War |
| | 13 June | Battle of Lowestoft – English victory |

	July	Outbreak of the Great Plague in London
	2 August	Skirmish at Bergen (Vågen) – Dutch victory
1666	January	France declares war on England
	11–14 June	Four Days Battle – draw
	4–5 August	St. James' Day Fight (North Foreland) – English victory
	August	'Holmes's Bonfire' – raid on Vlie Estuary
	September	Great Fire of London
1667	9–14 June	Raid on the Medway – Dutch victory
	July	Treaty of Breda – peace
1670	June	Treaty of Dover – secret Anglo-French alliance

1672–74 Third Anglo-Dutch War

1672	March	France declares war on Dutch
		English attack on Dutch convoy in English Channel
	April	Declaration of war
	7 June	Battle of Sole Bay – draw
1673	28 May & 4 June	Battle of Schooneveld – Dutch victory
	11 August	Battle of the Texel – Dutch victory
1674	February	Treaty of Westminster – peace
1685	February	Death of Charles II, accession of James, Duke of York as James II of England and VII of Scotland
1688	November	'Glorious Revolution' – Stadholder Willem van Oranje takes English throne
1689	February	Willem becomes King William III of England and II of Scotland.

The shipwright Peter Pett, pictured with his greatest creation, the powerful and ornate *Sovereign of the Seas*, which was launched at Woolwich in 1637. The *Sovereign* was the largest warship of both sides to see service during the Anglo-Dutch Wars. Painting by Sir Peter Lely (NMM BHC2949).

DESIGN AND DEVELOPMENT

Building a battle fleet of sailing warships was no easy matter. Expertise was required, along with shipyards, gun foundries, rope-makers, ironworkers, skilled shipwrights, experienced sailors, an efficient organization for naval supply and administration, and large quantities of natural resources – most of it timber. In 1652 only England and the Dutch Republic had sizeable battle fleets. Spain was undergoing a period of naval retrenchment and decline, while the French had yet to develop the infrastructure needed to build a large navy. In fact, they tended to rely on the Dutch to build their ships for them, either in Dutch shipyards, or through the hiring of Dutch shipwrights. With the possible exception of Denmark and Sweden, whose small fleets operated mainly in the Baltic, no European power could match the fleets ranged against each other across the North Sea.

The *Royal Sovereign* (formerly the *Sovereign of the Seas* or the *Sovereign*), as she appeared during the Third Anglo-Dutch War, when she flew the flag of Prince Rupert. In this detail of a painting attributed to Jacob Knyffe, the King's yacht, *Cleveland*, is shown alongside, during a royal visit to the flagship in June 1673 (Parker Gallery, London).

While the English and Dutch navies were broadly comparable in terms of size, they had very different roles, which in turn determined the nature and composition of the two fleets. The Dutch fleet evolved around the need to protect its merchant ships bound for the East Indies. This need for long-range warships, yet with the ability to negotiate the shallow coastal waters of their home coast, dictated the design of their warships. The English fleet developed from the large, powerful galleons of the Elizabethan and Jacobean eras, where firepower was considered all-important, and speed was increasingly sacrificed for reliability and strength.

As a result the ships of both nations were generally similar in appearance, but built according to different parameters, and therefore there were distinct national characteristics between the two fleets, at least at the start. The general trend during the period was towards standardization, and therefore the two national styles tended to converge, as the Dutch emulated the design

A **THE COMMONWEALTH: *NASEBY* (1652)**

The *Naseby* was the largest English warship built during the Commonwealth period. She was named after Parliament's decisive victory over the Royalists in 1645 – a floating political statement, reinforced by her figurehead, which depicted an equestrian Lord Protector Cromwell, riding over his vanquished enemies. Her long, lean appearance reflected the latest trends in warship design, and unlike many other large English warships of the period she was fast and manoeuvrable. With 80 heavy guns on three decks she was also extremely powerful. In 1660 she was renamed the *Royal Charles*, and in 1667 she suffered the indignity of being captured during the Dutch raid on the Medway.

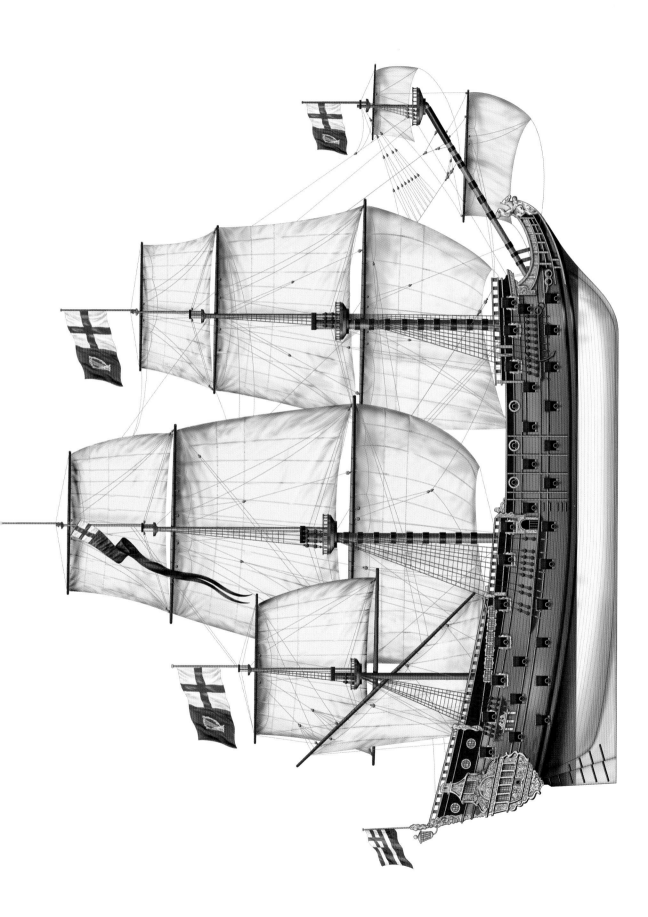

of English heavy ships, while still abiding by the constraints of draught and weight imposed by the need to operate in shallow water. Imitation was also common – in 1673 the English were so impressed by the French ship-of-the-line *Superbe* that they attempted to copy her design.

The basic fighting unit of both the Dutch and the English fleet was the ship-of-the-line, a warship that was strongly built and well armed, and therefore capable of holding her own in a line of battle. While these line of battle tactics were developed only during the First Anglo-Dutch War, the new tactic came about because of the ships themselves, as they carried their guns in large broadside batteries. It made perfect sense to try to make the most of this configuration, and hence the evolution of a tactical system which did just that. There was obviously a minimum size to a warship that could be expected to hold her own in a line of battle. In the First Anglo-Dutch War this was a ship of about 30 guns, but by the Third Anglo-Dutch War a warship of 40 guns was considered a weak link in the line. This was the result of a steady increase in firepower during the period, with all the consequences for ship design that this entailed.

English Ship Design

At the beginning of the First Anglo-Dutch War the English fleet was divided into two types of major warships – 'great ships' and 'frigates'. The great ship was what would become the ship-of-the-line, and had evolved from the race-built galleons that fought against the Spanish Armada in 1588. Since then they had evolved, becoming larger, higher and better armed. As a result they had lost something of their manoeuvrability and the great ships of the early seventeenth century had a reputation for being slow and lumbering – a far cry from the Elizabethan race-built galleon. Still, English shipbuilders such as Phineas Pett and William Burrell did what they could to produce useful and relatively manoeuvrable warships.

The three Elizabethan galleons that still remained in the fleet in 1652 had all been extensively modified to conform to the new emphasis on armament rather than sailing performance. In addition ten great ships had been built in the royal shipyards of Deptford and Woolwich between 1618 and 1634. Despite some reservations these Jacobean and Carolean vessels generally met with approval, largely because of their heavy armament and impressively stout construction. Nine of them were still in service in 1652, and five remained in the fleet throughout all three Anglo-Dutch Wars. This somewhat belies their reputation for lack of manoeuvrability, although ease of handling seems to have been less important than their ability to fight effectively in a line of battle. In that kind of sea battle, their stout construction proved a godsend.

Then in 1634 King Charles ordered the construction of a revolutionary new vessel –

HMS *Mary*, formerly the Commonwealth 'frigate' *Speaker*. This successful Third Rate was the first of a class of 13 similar warships. The *Speaker/Mary* fought in all the major non-Mediterranean battles of the three Anglo-Dutch Wars. Engraving by Willem van de Velde the Elder.

a ship-of-the-line so large and imposing that she was called *Sovereign of the Seas*. Her great size and heavy armament might have made her slow and difficult to manoeuvre, but instead she handled well, and proved a great success. This was largely thanks to the skill of her designer, Peter Pett, who succeeded his father as a master shipwright, and who was prepared to experiment with hull shape and layout in order to produce a better design of warship. She was a three-decker, meaning that she carried her guns on two near-continuous lower gun decks, as well as on her upper deck. This represented a departure in English ship design as, apart from the *Royal Prince* of 1610, the emphasis had hitherto been on smaller warships that could `combine an impressive amount of firepower with some modicum of manoeuvrability. Pett rewrote the manual on warship design by creating a ship in which handling and performance were no longer considered secondary to firepower. Instead the *Sovereign of the Seas* might have been an enormous floating gun battery, but she was one that consistently impressed observers with her ability to manoeuvre.

The largest English warship built during the Jacobean period, the powerful Second Rate *Triumph*, built in 1623, played an active part in all three of the Anglo-Dutch Wars. At the battles of Dungeness and Portland she served as the flagship of Admiral Blake. Engraving by Willem van de Velde the Elder.

This great ship also led to a new tactical notion, that a warship could win a sea battle through firepower alone, rather than through a combination of fire and movement. In essence, her manoeuvrability was useful while she reached the optimum position to fire on the enemy, but from that point on manoeuvre was secondary, and firepower was seen as the arbiter of victory. While the line of battle had yet to be invented, the *Sovereign of the Seas* represented an important step in the development of the ship-of-the-line. She also cost so much to build that Charles had to impose a ship tax (Ship Money) on his population – a levy that played a major part in the growing unrest that led to the outbreak of Civil War, and ultimately to Charles's defeat and execution.

During the English Civil War (1642–46) the bulk of the navy declared their allegiance to Parliament. Its great ships were really designed to fight their European counterparts, and so they proved unsuited to the lesser tasks of chasing Royalist privateers or blockading Royalist-held ports. Instead the navy hired smaller, lighter-armed vessels from Dunkirk, or turned captured Royalist privateers against their former owners. This policy continued during the First Anglo-Dutch War, as the Commonwealth boosted their regular fleet through the temporary commissioning of prizes, privateers or armed merchantmen. It was only in 1645 that the first English-built privateer – the *Constant Warwick* – was hired and then brought into service. This fast, light, but powerful vessel formed the basis of a new warship – the frigate. She was described as an 'incomparable sailer' by her captain, and within months Parliament commissioned the building of three frigates of its own – the *Assurance*, *Adventure* and *Nonsuch*.

By 1649 the Commonwealth Navy had eight frigates in service, with more on order. However, experience showed that these warships were too small for extended operations far from their home ports. Consequently Parliament commissioned a new series of larger frigates, and so began blurring the distinction between great ship and frigate. While the ships of the resulting Speaker class were technically classed as frigates, they were two-deckers, and carried an armament comparable with a great ship. This made them too useful to waste on commerce raiding, privateer hunting or escort duties. Instead, their manoeuvrability and firepower was needed to augment the main battle fleet. These Speaker class frigates, together with the even larger 'great frigate', *Antelope*, were distinguishable from contemporary great ships only by their longer, narrower hulls, and their lower superstructure.

This English experiment with frigates was short-lived. While more than 40 were built under the Commonwealth, thanks to the lessons learned during the First Anglo-Dutch War the emphasis had shifted once again, from a warship that combined firepower and manoeuvrability to larger, more ponderous warships, capable of carrying larger and heavier batteries of ordnance. Therefore after the Restoration of 1660, the frigate-building programme was abandoned, and instead the Admiralty concentrated its resources on the development of larger warships. This emphasis would continue throughout the period, culminating in the great 90–100 gun warships produced during the late 1660s and early 1670s.

Therefore, the great ships that were considered of little value before the First Anglo-Dutch War suddenly became the arbiters of naval victory. It was

TOP
The *Adventure*, built in Woolwich by Peter Pett the Younger, was one of the first frigates to enter service in the English fleet – a Fourth Rate based on the successful design of the privateer *Constant Warwick*. Engraving by Willem van de Velde the Elder.

BELOW
A Third Rate English warship of the early Restoration period, believed to be the *Rupert* of 66 guns, built at Harwich in 1666. She fought in the Four Days Battle and St. James' Day Fight of 1666, and later at Sole Bay (1672) and Shooneveld (1673). Engraving by Willem van de Velde the Younger.

just as well that during the Civil War the Navy Board resisted Parliamentarian pressure to cut the existing fleet of great ships down, and to convert them into lighter and more manoeuvrable warships. Instead these great ships of the Jacobean and Carolean navy remained, in case of intervention by another European power and to 'maintain the honour of the sea'. In a move that flew in the face of this pressure, during the decade before the start of the First Anglo-Dutch War the Parliamentarian Navy Board ordered that many of these warships were modified to carry more guns, which naturally made them even less manoeuvrable than before. For instance, the *George* was designed to carry 42 guns, but by 1652 she had been reconfigured to carry 52 pieces, achieved by covering over her spar deck, and so converting her into a three-decker. Similarly the *Prince* was reconfigured to carry 100 guns, rather than the 70 she had originally been designed for. This, though, made her unwieldy, and by 1652 her armament had been reduced to 80 guns.

An exception to this policy of upgrading was the *Sovereign*, formerly the *Sovereign of the Seas*. Her forecastle and sterncastle were lowered and shortened, the gratings over her upper deck were removed, and much of her grand decoration was removed. In effect the Carolean flagship became just another great ship, albeit a particularly large and majestic one. Like the rest of the fleet, the aim was to turn these ships into floating gun batteries, and any alteration of their seakeeping qualities or manoeuvrability was of secondary importance.

It is often assumed that the practice of rating sailing warships according to the size of their gun batteries was a result of the new line of battle tactics.

The First Rate HMS *Royal Charles* of 80 guns, formerly the *Naseby*, was one of the most powerful warships in the English fleet at the start of the Second Anglo-Dutch War. However, she was captured by the Dutch during the raid on the Medway (1667), and towed back to Holland. Due to her deep draught the Dutch were unable to add her to their fleet. Detail of a painting attributed to Isaac Sailmaker (Bristol Museum and Art Gallery).

In fact, the system was in use before the Civil War, when great ships were divided into three ranks: First Rank, which was reserved for *Sovereign of the Seas*; Second Rank, which consisted of the larger great ships; and Third Rank, which contained the smaller 'middling ships' or great ships of less than 500 tons and 32 guns. Fleet orders issued in the spring of 1653 make no reference to rating, and even the term 'frigate' seemed to be applied inconsistently, as the larger frigates were grouped alongside other 'middling' or 'great ships'.

By the start of the Second Dutch War the rating system was in unofficial use, and it was officially adopted before the outbreak of the Third Anglo-Dutch War. However, this adoption had more to do with pay scales and manning levels than any rigid categorization by means of tonnage or armament. The divisions were largely subjective, and essentially great ships became First or Second Rates, middling ships and frigates were classed as Third or Fourth Rates, and smaller warships were either Fifth Rates, Sixth Rates or were classed as unrated.

The Restoration emphasis on large warships was actually a continuation of a Commonwealth shipbuilding programme, in which a series of four warships were built, the largest of which was the *Naseby*, with 80 guns. This programme was continued after the Restoration, with the building of the Second Rates *Royal Oak* and *Royal Katherine*, followed in 1666 by the *Loyal London*, which, like the *Royal Oak*, was destroyed by fire in 1667. As the Restoration Admiralty shunned the advice of anyone tainted by Republicanism, none of these new large ships was particularly successful. The *Royal Katherine* in particular was singled out as a failure, and as Samuel Pepys pointed out, 'her lower ports are but three feet above water before she hath all her provisions and guns in'. She was designed by Christopher Pett, the nephew of Peter, who evidently lacked the sure hand of his uncle. Incidentally, in some

HMS *St. Andrew* built by Christopher Pett was one of seven English First or Second Rates built between the Second and Third Anglo-Dutch Wars. Like her near sisters the *London* and the *Charles*, she was manoeuvrable as well as powerfully armed. Painting by Willem van de Velde the Elder (NMM BHC3618).

accounts, both of these first two warships were described as frigate, although by any definition they were fully fledged ships-of-the-line.

Another budding shipwright of the period was Anthony Deane, who became Master Shipwright at Harwich in 1664. Later that year he was commissioned to build a new Third Rate called the *Rupert* 'of the size and dimensions of the *Mary* [formerly the *Speaker*] frigate'. When completed the *Rupert* was larger than the *Mary*, thanks to the influence of Peter Pett, now Commissioner of the royal dockyard at Chatham. Both the elderly Pett and the younger Deane produced a design that would mirror the performance of the Speaker class before they were overburdened with extra guns. However, these new ships would be both well armed and manoeuvrable, and purpose-built to stand in a line of battle. Three more smaller Fourth Rates were also designed along similar lines.

The experience of the Second Anglo-Dutch War led to another rethink of English warship design. The fleet also had to make up the loss of some of its largest ships during the raid on the Medway (1667). The result was a spate of post-war ship construction, with the commissioning of three First Rates (*Prince*, *Royal James* and *Royal Charles*), plus four Second Rates (*St. Michael*, *London*, *Charles* and *St. Andrew*) and two Third Rates (*Resolution* and *Edgar*). Dean was involved in the design of all three groups of ships, and took a direct hand in the building of three of them – *Royal James*, *Royal Charles* and *Resolution*. In fact these Second Rates were effectively First Rates, as they carried more than 90 guns.

When John Tippets built the *St. Michael* he, like Dean before him, exceeded his brief, and produced a larger warship than had originally been intended. The charred hull of the *Loyal London* was rebuilt as the *London* in 1670,

In this painting by Willem Van de Velde the Younger the *Hollandia* (80 guns) is seen in action during the battle of the Texel (1673). During the battle she flew the flag of Cornelis Tromp, who commanded the Dutch rearguard. Note the double tricolour variant of the usual ensign of the United Provinces(NMM BHC0315).

and effectively became another First Rate, while the *Charles* and the *St. Andrew* were both reclassified as First Rates before the outbreak of the Third Anglo-Dutch War. In effect the Second Rate had ceased to exist, as there was now no real difference between the two larger rating groups. This all reflected a trend to build bigger and better warships, creating a battle fleet that was as powerful as the Admiralty could possibly make it.

In effect they were building First Rates, but for political reasons they downplayed the size and composition of these new warships. Conversely the Fourth Rates of the fleet had fallen from favour. These were the 50-gun

THE RESTORATION: HMS *ST. ANDREW* (1673)

The *St. Andrew* was built in Woolwich under the guidance of Christopher Pett, and she entered service in 1670. This 1,338 ton warship carried 96 guns, and although planned as a Second Rate, she was soon reclassified as a First Rate flagship. Her lines drew on the experience gained during the two previous Anglo-Dutch Wars, and by all accounts she was an extremely successful design. Her unusually wide beam aided her stability as a gun platform. She was so well thought of that a class of post-war Second Rates were based on her, becoming effectively scaled-down versions of the larger original.

During the Third Anglo-Dutch War she flew the flag of Rear-Admiral Sir John Kempthorne, and like most First Rates she saw more action than many smaller warships. She served with distinction at the battles of Solebay, Schooneveld and the Texel. She remained in service after the war, and went on to see action at Beachy Head (1690) and Barfleur (1692) before being completely rebuilt as the *Royal Anne* in 1703. She was finally broken up in 1727.

HMS *St. Andrew* (First Rate)
Built: 1670 Tonnage: 1,338
Armament: 96 guns (26 42-pdrs, 26 18-pdrs, 28 9-pdrs, 16 6-pdrs)
Dimensions: Keel Length: 129 feet Beam: 43 feet 6 inches Draught: 18 feet 8 inches

One of several Dutch warships to share the name, this *Eendracht* of 70 guns blew up during her first engagement, the battle of Lowestoft (1665). In this engraving by Willem van de Velde the Elder a council of war is being held aboard her before the battle. (Maritime Museum Prins Hendrik, Rotterdam)

warships – mainly frigates – that had formed the backbone of the Commonwealth Navy. At the time of the Restoration in 1660 some 45 of them were in service – a total that had dropped to just 24 two decades later. It was generally assumed that these smaller warships were of less value than the imposing First Rates, which could tower over the enemy, and it was now expected that in time of war these smaller rated warships could be augmented by armed merchantmen, or enemy prizes.

By the end of the Third Dutch War the English fleet had developed into a powerful naval force, but one that was only comparable with the newly raised French fleet, and slightly inferior in numbers to the Dutch navy. It was clear that in order to maintain the size and effectiveness of the Royal Navy a major shipbuilding programme needed to be implemented, and this is exactly what happened. Anthony Deane – now Sir Anthony – was the architect of this new shipbuilding initiative, which became known as the 1677 Programme. While it and the ships that were built as a result lie beyond the scope of this book, it is worth noting that Deane seized this opportunity to build a more balanced fleet, with new warships being built in all major rating groups. This, then, was the real legacy of the Anglo-Dutch Wars – a Royal Naval battle fleet that consisted of well-rounded and well-built ships, whose designs were based on the hard-won experience of three major naval conflicts.

Dutch Ship Design

In theory the Dutch had a powerful navy. It had been forged in battle against the Spanish, playing its part in the Dutch Revolt (or Eighty Years War) and so helping to secure independence for the Republic. The Dutch fleet inflicted a decisive defeat on the Spanish at the battle of the Downs (1639), an achievement that highlighted the superiority of Dutch ship design and tactical thinking. To be fair, the Dutch fleet greatly outnumbered the Spaniards, but only two of the Dutch ships carried more than 40 guns. Apart from the 42-gun *Maeght van Dordrecht* and the Dutch flagship *Aemelia* (56 guns) the majority of the Dutch vessels were small, and carried no more than 24–30 guns apiece.

The Dutch had no established state shipbuilding policy, and instead the Republic relied on the cooperation of several largely independent Admiralties, supported by makeshift warships pressed into service from the Vereenigde Oost-Indische Compagnie ('VOC', the Dutch East India Company) or the smaller Geoctroyeerde Westindische Compagnie ('GWIC', the Dutch West India Company). Some of these Indiamen, particularly the biggest VOC ships, were larger than most Dutch warships of the period, and carried as many as 70 guns. They looked little different from contemporary Dutch warships, but if anything their hulls were more stoutly constructed, to better weather the storms of the Atlantic or Indian Oceans. The drawback with Indiamen was that the guns themselves tended to be lighter than those carried on conventional Dutch warships.

This political and administrative division would continue throughout the Anglo-Dutch Wars. In 1652 the Republican party held power in the Netherlands; they were politically opposed to the expansion of central authority in the country. Instead Dutch sovereignty rested in the hands of a federation of smaller semi-autonomous states, an arrangement reflected in the official name of the new country, the Republic of the Seven United Provinces. More commonly the country was known as the United Netherlands, or the United Provinces. Each of the five maritime provinces had its own Admiralty, and was responsible for its own maritime defence. These Admiralties of Amsterdam, the Maas (Rotterdam), Zeeland, Friesland and the North Quarter were also expected to supply ships, supplies and men for a combined fleet. Of these Admiralties, Amsterdam and the Maas were by far the most important, as they maintained the largest provincial fleets.

The reason that small ships were favoured by these provincial admiralties was partly due to historical circumstance, and partly thanks to geography. Historically, during the Eighty Years War the Dutch provinces had joined forces to send privateering fleets to harry the Spanish in the Caribbean, and these smaller warships remained in widespread use until after the end of the First Anglo-Dutch War in 1654. Geographically, the Dutch also suffered from the limitations imposed by their shallow coastal waters. This meant that with a few exceptions, the majority of Dutch warships of this period were shallow-draughted, and drew no more than 15 feet of water – the equivalent of an English Fourth Rate. This imposed a major constraint on Dutch warship design, and led to the tendency of Dutch ships to have flatter bottoms and broader beams than their English counterparts. This at least had the advantage of making them stable gun platforms, although the Dutch never favoured the overloading of warships with guns, as they rightly saw that this degraded their performance and manoeuvrability.

In 1652 the Dutch were able to field a fleet of 112 ships, a combination of warships of the five maritime provinces, Indiamen pressed into service of the Republic, and armed merchantmen, hired for the duration of hostilities. This total increased to almost 150 ships following the return of the East Indies fleet.

The sterns of the majority of Dutch warships of this period were decorated with a combination of gilding and carving, usually painted in gold leaf, as well as by painted scenes or emblems above them on the stern transom. This engraving shows the *Brederode*, at the battle of the Gabbard, 1652. Detail of an engraving by Heerman Witmont.

The small 300-ton Dutch warship *Harderwijk* built by the Amsterdam Admiralty in 1662 carried her 40 guns on two decks. She took part in all the major battles of the Second Anglo-Dutch War. Engraving by Willem van de Velde the Elder.

Inevitably, the stern decoration of the *Gouden Leeuw* ('Golden Lion') of the Amsterdam Admiralty reflected her name. This sister ship of the *Witte Olifant* was a three-decker of 82 guns. Detail of a painting by Willem van de Velde the Younger, showing her at anchor off Amsterdam (Rijksmuseum, Amsterdam).

The size of the Dutch fleet remained remarkably constant throughout the three Anglo-Dutch conflicts, with 139 remaining in service by the end of the third war. Each province (sometimes confusingly called a 'republic') maintained its own shipyards, and adopted its own approach towards design and construction. Economic necessity dictated that the peacetime size of each of these fleets be kept relatively small, but another Dutch policy designed to assist in the cost of running these fleets was the practice of using warships as merchantmen when their naval services weren't required. The shipyards were used to building merchant ships, and therefore the vessels they produced were more lightly constructed than their stoutly built English counterparts. This made them more manoeuvrable, but also more vulnerable to damage from enemy gunfire.

This approach to ship design was appropriate for a war against the Spanish, who lacked the ships to counter the Dutch, but the naval conflict against England in 1652–54 exposed the weakness of the policy. The Dutch were unable to match the firepower or resilience of the English warships, particularly after the English adopted their new line of battle tactics. It was evident that a more conjoined approach to ship design was needed before the fleet could fight the English on anything like equal terms. A two-tiered approach was adopted. First, the five maritime provinces would embark on their own shipbuilding programme, where the emphasis would be on constructing large purpose-built warships, capable of holding their place in a line of battle.

These ships would be stoutly constructed, or at least more stoutly built than before. In all some 60 of these new warships would enter service before the start of the next war. Until they entered service the Indiamen remained the largest warships in Dutch service. During the Second Anglo-Dutch War they

C

EARLY DUTCH: *BREDERODE* (1653)

The *Brederode* was the fleet flagship of the Dutch navy during the First Anglo-Dutch War, at various times flying the flag of Admiral Maarten Tromp and Admiral Michiel de Ruyter. She was by far the largest and best-armed warship in the Dutch fleet during the conflict. Named by the Maas Admiralty after Johan van Brederode, the brother-in-law of the Prince of Orange, this powerful 56-gun ship was built in Rotterdam in 1646, under the guidance of Master Shipwright Jan Salomonszoon van den Tempel. During the First Anglo-Dutch War she took part in the first clash off Dover (1652), followed by the battles of Kentish Knock and Dungeness in 1652, followed by Gabbard and Scheveningen in 1653. She survived the war, despite being in the thick of the fighting, although Admiral Tromp was killed on board during the final battle off Scheveningen. She was finally lost in action against the Swedes during the battle of the Sound in 1658.

Brederode (Third Rate)
Built: 1646 Tonnage: 920
Armament: 54 guns (4 36-pdrs, 12 24-pdrs, 8 18-pdrs, 20 12-pdrs, 10 6-pdrs)
Dimensions: Keel Length: 132 feet Beam: 32 feet Draught: 13 feet 5 inches

were called to the colours again, but they suffered disproportionately heavy losses during the early fighting, particularly at the battle of Lowestoft (1665), and by 1666 very few remained in the fleet. After all, their loss would represent a severe financial blow to the Dutch economy, and those that remained needed to be protected so they could resume their lucrative work after the peace.

Another particularly Dutch feature was the use of a square transom, or flat stern. By contrast English warships favoured a more hydrodynamically efficient rounded stern. The reason was economic rather than anything else, as square-transomed ships were quicker and cheaper to build. In the bows the Dutch had a less pronounced 'cutwater' or forward curve of the bow than did their English counterparts. Again this was done to reduce shipbuilding time and expense. By the time of the Third Anglo-Dutch War newly built Dutch warships had a bluff bow, rather than the long graceful beak favoured during previous decades.

Another feature of these new, purpose-built Dutch warships was the almost complete lack of decoration, save from at the stern. Most of them carried a figurehead, usually a red or gold-painted lion, the symbol of the Dutch Republic. While English warships of the Commonwealth period were equally subdued, Restoration warships put their Dutch counterparts to shame in terms of embellishment. The Dutch didn't encircle their upper-deck gunports in carved wooden wreaths, and their sterncastles were decorated simply, save for carvings surrounding the great cabin. Instead, decoration was concentrated aft, with Dutch or provincial coats of arms, carvings of figures, and reasonably muted carvings surmounting the stern transom. These stern transoms were also painted with scenes reflecting the name, home port or province of the ship, often by well-known contemporary Dutch artists.

The result of this shipbuilding programme was that the Dutch commenced the Second Anglo-Dutch War with a far more balanced fleet than before, and one that was on numerical parity with the Royal Navy. For the most part this fleet was composed of pure-bred warships. Hastily converted merchantmen would no longer form the bulk of the fleet. Instead the smaller, older warships would augment a central group of these new large warships – the flagships of each provincial fleet. By Dutch standards these core warships were large two-deckers, carrying 60–70 guns apiece. The largest of them, the *Hollandia*, was an 80-gun warship, the equivalent of an English Second Rate. By the end of the war no fewer than 11 70- or 80-gun ships were in Dutch service. The largest of them, the Amsterdam-built warships *Gouden Dolfin* (86 guns) and the 82-gun *Gouden Leeuw* and *Witte Olifant* were actually three-deckers, as the waists of the vessels had been decked over to provide more space for the guns. The trouble was, with the exception of Indiamen, most of the older smaller ships were the equivalent of English Fourth Rates, carrying less than 50 guns apiece.

While these large Second Rate ships were still relatively few in number, they were the equal of the larger units of the English fleet, although still not as stoutly constructed as the ships of their foes. Just as importantly they were both faster and more manoeuvrable than their English counterparts – advantages that proved their worth in battle. Their

The stern of the English warship *Garland*, built in 1620. She carries the emblem of the English Commonwealth in her stern – a crest showing the Irish harp and the cross of St George. The 40-gun *Garland* was captured at the battle of Dungeness (1652), and recaptured the following year at the battle of Scheveningen. Engraving by Willem van de Velde the Elder.

weakness lay in firepower. Because of the requirement to limit their draught, Dutch warships tended to carry lighter guns than their equivalent English counterparts, which limited their offensive punch. However, it can be argued that the smaller guns had a slightly higher rate of fire, which may have gone some way to compensating for their lack of calibre.

Samuel Pepys said of these new Dutch warships that they were built 'with two decks, which carried from 60 to 70 guns, and were so contrived that they carried their lower guns four foot from the water, and to stow four months provisions'. Like previous Dutch warships, their wide beam compensated for their shallow draught, and made them stable gun platforms. This limitation of draught was the only reason the Dutch avoided building large First Rate warships. A vessel the size of the *Hollandia* was the largest that could be constructed, and even she was limited to operating from Dutch ports such as Amsterdam, where the water was deep enough to accommodate a vessel of her size.

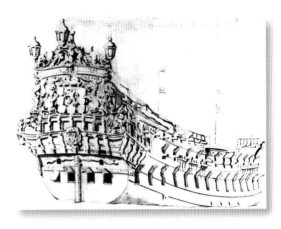

The *Zeven Provincien* ('Seven Provinces') was the largest warship in the Dutch fleet during the Second Anglo-Dutch War. She played a prominent part in the Four Days Battle and the St. James' Day Fight in 1666, the battle of Felixstowe (1667) and at the battle of Schooneveld (1673). Engraving by Willem van de Velde the Younger.

After the end of the Second Anglo-Dutch War the spate of new ship construction came to an end. Instead the Dutch were forced to concentrate the resources of the state on improving the army, so it was better able to face the threat posed by King Louis XIV of France. Consequently no major ship construction was undertaken before 1672, which meant that the Dutch fleet of the Third Anglo-Dutch War was largely the same as the one that fought in the previous conflict. The Dutch therefore faced the same problem as before – fighting an opponent who had larger and more powerful warships than their own. As before, the Dutch made up for this deficiency through the superior quality of their commanders, and the skill of their seamen. In the end it was this skill that allowed the Dutch to hold their own in these last two conflicts and to emerge from the Anglo-Dutch Wars with the reputation of their navy intact.

CONSTRUCTION AND OPERATION

Shipbuilding

It has often been said that the large sailing ship of war was the most complex man-made structure produced before the start of the Industrial Revolution. Commissioning a new ship was a serious business, as it involved the expenditure of considerable time, money and effort. For the most part the major warships that fought in the three Anglo-Dutch Wars were built in specialist dockyards, either the five royal dockyards in England (Chatham, Deptford, Harwich, Portsmouth or Woolwich), or in the nine Dutch provincial Admiralty dockyards (Amsterdam, Enkhizen, Harlingen, Hoorn, Medemblik, Middelburg, Rotterdam or Vlissingen). There were exceptions of course. Smaller warships – even some frigates – were built in more modest private shipyards, while the Dutch East India Company maintained its own shipbuilding facilities, based in Amsterdam.

The time taken to build a sailing ship of war varied, with the Dutch frequently completing and fitting out ships within a year, while the English yards often took twice that time, or even longer. The difference was partly the result of better Dutch administration and shipyard organization, the all too frequent dearth of funds in the English treasury, and the fact that Dutch

HMS *Royal Katherine* was one of three Second Rates built during the years immediately following the Restoration, and saw action during most of the battles of the last two Anglo-Dutch conflicts. Despite her longevity of service, she was viewed as a badly designed ship. Painting by H. Vale (NMM BHC3606).

ships tended to be less solidly constructed than their English counterparts. As each of the three wars lasted less than three years, there was barely time to add wartime vessels to the fleet. Therefore ships tended to be built in time of peace, and in wartime the dockyards were given over to the completion of existing ships, or the repair of those damaged in battle. For much of the time the bulk of the 'fleet in being' was maintained 'in ordinary' – the ships decommissioned, de-rigged, manned by skeleton crews and kept in reserve, ready for when they were needed. This was particularly true of the larger warships in both fleets, which had little or no role to play in a peacetime navy.

D

LATER DUTCH: *EENDRACHT* (1666) AND *GOUDEN LEEUW* (1672)

The *Eendracht* (top) was one of two flagships of the Maas Admiralty to bear the name, and no fewer than ten warships named *Eendracht* (meaning 'unity' or 'concord') took part in the three Dutch wars. This particular *Eendracht* was built in Dordrecht during 1653 by van den Tempel, but she was completed too late to take part in the First Anglo-Dutch War. The *Eendracht* carried 58 guns, although the total was increased to 76 shortly before the start of the Second Anglo-Dutch conflict. She served as the fleet flagship of Admiral van Opdam at the battle of the Sound (1658) fought against the Swedes, and she performed the same function for van Opdam at the battle of Lowestoft (1665). During the battle she was attacked by the *Royal Charles* (formerly the *Naseby*). The reason is still unclear, but the *Eendracht* suddenly blew up, claiming the lives of van Opdam and virtually her entire 400 man crew. Within a year a second *Eendracht* was commissioned, and she took part in the remaining battles of the war.

The *Gouden Leeuw* ('Golden Lion', below) of 80 guns was built by the Amsterdam Admiralty in 1666, and equipped by the Dutch East India Company. As the flagship of Lieutenant-Admiral (Vice-Admiral) Cornelis Tromp she took part in the Four Days Battle and the St. James' Day Fight of 1666. She was a large warship by Dutch standards – almost a three-decker, as she carried a large battery in her forecastle and sterncastle.

With only minor exceptions there was no real difference between English and Dutch shipbuilding practices – only the ships themselves varied. The basic specifications of the new warship – her size, dimensions, strength of construction, size and placement of gun batteries and stores, and her maximum draught were all laid down by the Admiralty, whether English or Dutch provincial. The Master Shipwright of the dockyard would then produce plans – construction draughts – and sometimes a ship model. However, he was given leeway to design and build the ship as he liked, within the parameters set down by the Admiralty. That meant that even ships of the same class, and of the same specifications, might be slightly different from each other.

The next problem was the supply of material. A large ship-of-the-line might need as many as 3,000 trees to be felled for her construction. Timber had to be stockpiled – shipped in from German forests in the case of the Dutch, or from the New Forest or the Forest of Dean for English building projects. Long straight pine trees for masts and spars were imported from Russia, Scandinavia or, for use in England, from the American colonies. The shipbuilders also needed metal fittings, wooden treenails, canvas, tar and a host of other materials. All these had to be transported to the dockyard by land or sea, and the timber had to be seasoned for two or three years to dry the sap. This meant that busy dockyards had to be well stocked, ready for any future commissions.

Space in this book precludes a detailed account of warship construction during this period. Suffice it to say the building of a naval vessel followed time-honoured lines, and was extremely labour intensive, despite the use of semi-mechanical aids such as horse- or water-powered sawmills or cranes. Construction began with the laying of the keel – the backbone of the ship – which was usually formed from several sections. The frames or ribs were added, to create the basic skeleton of the ship. Again, these curved timbers, which provided shape to the hull, were composed of several sections. Longitudinal timbers – wales – were laid across these, to provide strength, and to produce a cohesive hull structure. It was common to leave a ship in this state – known as 'in frame' - for several months, to give the timber yet more time to season.

Then the ship was planked, with horizontal planks attached to the outside of the frames. An inner layer or ceiling was then attached to the inside of the frames. These frames and planks were tapered off towards the bow, and also towards the stern in English ships, at least below the waterline. The transom stern was added – an essentially flat surface, attached to the sternpost, and to the last frames of the hull. This was designed to hold the rudder, and to house

One of the larger Dutch warships of the Second Anglo-Dutch War, the *Witte Olifant* ('White Elephant') was built by the Amsterdam Admiralty, and carried her 82 guns on three decks. Engraving by Willem van de Velde the Elder.

what would become the stern and quarter galleries surrounding the great cabin. At the other end of the vessel the shape of the cutwater at the bow varied depending on nationality, but essentially it ended in a curved stempost that was linked to the hull proper and the foremost frame by a beakhead. These foremost frames were also closed off by adding a transverse bulkhead, or beakhead bulkhead.

With the hull completed the ship was decked over, the deck timbers resting on transverse beams, which in turn rested on wooden knees that resembled the brackets of a modern shelf. Typically, the area below the lowest deck or orlop deck became the hold, where the ship's ballast and stores were kept, and the rear of this deck – below the quarterdeck – became the cockpit, used as a surgery ward during an action. Beneath it lay the magazine, sited well below the waterline. Above the orlop were the gun decks, the number depending on the size of the ship. Above these was the upper deck,

This powerful Dutch two-decker has been tentatively identified as the *Vrijheid*, built in Amsterdam in 1651, and which flew the flag of Vice-Admiral de With during the Second Anglo-Dutch War. Detail of a grisaille by Willem van de Velde the Elder.

which could be completely planked over, or might be open in the waist, creating a spar deck, that allowed easy ventilation of the gun deck below.

Above the upper deck were the forecastle forward, and the quarterdeck aft. The latter was the preserve of the ship's officers, and the command area when at sea. Towards the stern of this could be an additional poop deck, built over a cabin structure known as a roundhouse. Decoration could be added, but on Dutch or Commonwealth ships this was reasonably muted compared to the earlier Stuart period or the Restoration. In both navies the figurehead was usually a lion, while vertical headpieces – usually in the form of statuary of humans or animals surrounded the stern and quarter galleries. Apart from the wreathed upper-deck gunports of English ships, the bulk of the decoration was saved for the stern transom, which was usually carved with a coat of arms – the arms of the Commonwealth, the English royal coat of arms, or the emblem of the Dutch Republic or relevant province. The baroque influence was noticeable, particularly in the carvings surmounting the stern transom.

When the ship was finished save for the addition of the masts she was launched, having already received her name. While many Commonwealth ships were named after republican virtues, or Parliamentarian victories, in the fleet of Charles II names tended to reflect the glory of the crown or the kingdom. Any ships with overtly republican names were duly renamed in 1660. Traditional English ship names such as *Triumph*, *Vanguard* or *Revenge* were also popular. In the Netherlands the tendency was to name ships after towns or provinces, civic ideals such as unity (*eendracht*), peace (*vrede*) or love (*liefde*), or the coat of arms of a particular province. Painted stern decoration tended to reflect the ship's name.

After launching, the ship was fitted out with masts, spars, sails and rigging, moved to an ordnance wharf to receive her guns and ordnance stores,

E THE *SOVEREIGN* (1652)

By any standards the *Sovereign of the Seas* was a remarkable warship. She was built on the express orders of King Charles I by Peter Pett, the Master Shipwright at Woolwich. Many doubted such a large warship could be built, but Pett proved them wrong, and the immense 1,500-ton vessel was launched in October 1637, after three years of construction. She was the most expensive warship in the world – her gilding and decoration alone cost almost £7,000, having been lavishly created by the playwright and stage set designer Thomas Heywood. Remarkably, despite her great size, this leviathan proved a reliable, manoeuvrable and seaworthy warship. However, what really set her apart was her armament of 106 guns, which gave her a broadside weight of more than 1,000 pounds – a real ship-smashing salvo.

During the English Civil War she lay in reserve in the River Medway, but was refitted in 1651, and renamed the *Sovereign*. As Admiral Blake's flagship she first fired her vast broadside in anger in October 1652, during the battle of Kentish Knock, carving her way through the Dutch fleet and causing so much damage that her foes called her 'De Gouden Deivel' (The Golden Devil). The *Sovereign* was rebuilt in 1660, and went on to fight with distinction during the next two Anglo-Dutch wars, and at the battles of Beachy Head (1690), Barfleur and La Hogue (1692). She was finally destroyed in an accidental fire while anchored off Chatham in 1696. In this plate she is depicted as she would have looked during the battle of Kentish Knock.

Key

1   Anchor and Cathead
2   Stem and Cutwater
3   Forecastle
4   Beakhead
5   Figurehead
6   Bowsprit
7   Spritsail Topmast and Jackstaff
8   Foremast
9   Upper Deck (also waist, and upper gundeck)
10 Middle Deck (also middle gundeck)
11 Mainmast
12 Quarterdeck
13 Mizzenmast
14 Poop Deck
15 Ensign Staff
16 Stern Lanterns
17 Quarter Gallery
18 Great Cabin
19 Stern Gallery
20 Quarter and Stern decoration
21 Lower Great Cabin
22 Rudder
23 Admiral's Quarters
24 Gunroom
25 Deadwood
26 Ballast
27 Cockpit
28 Shot Locker and After Hold
29 Main well and chain pumps
30 Capstan
31 Main hold
32 Orlop Deck and Cable Tier
33 Storerooms
34 Lower Deck (also lower gundeck)

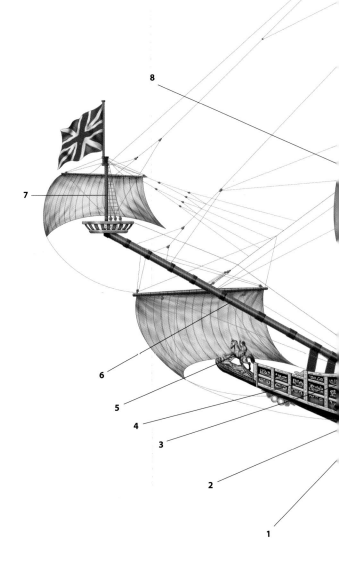

Lieutenant-Admiral Maarten Tromp (1598–1653) commanded the Dutch fleet during the First Anglo-Dutch War, and is generally regarded as the best Dutch naval commander of the period. His death at the battle of Scheveningen was a grievous blow to the Dutch cause (Rijksmuseum, Amsterdam).

then crewed and provisioned. Finally the new vessel was ready for service, even if this might only be a few voyages to test its performance, and then being placed into the reserve fleet, to save on peacetime expenditure. During her operational life the warship would be brought into a dockyard to be repaired, to have minor refits made such as the repair of worn timbers, and occasionally to undergo a thorough refit and modernization. In time of war the dockyard would also be responsible for bringing a ship out of reserve, and preparing her for active service – a process that could take as long as three months. In peacetime the dockyards were able to plan these refits around the building of new ships and other essential work. In time of war they were hard-pressed to cope with the sudden demands placed upon them – preparing a fleet for sea, and repairing the battle damage to active warships, or to enemy prizes.

Manpower

During the years preceding the First Dutch War the Commonwealth virtually doubled the size of its navy. In addition, some 100 vessels were added to the navy list, either hired merchantmen or else prizes captured from the Dutch or the Royalists. Inevitably there were problems finding the crewmen needed to man the ships. Another problem was disaffection, which was largely the result of a Parliamentarian purge of political or religious malcontents within the fleet. This led to a widespread mutiny in 1649, which caused the defection of several ships and crews to the Royalist privateering squadron, then operating under the command of Prince Rupert. The Commonwealth response to this crisis was to reorganize the fleet – a 'New Modelling' in line with the earlier reform of the army. This only proved effective when it was matched by a similar reorganization of pay and conditions.

Lieutenant-Admiral Michiel de Ruyter (1607–1676) learned his trade during the First Anglo-Dutch War, and then led the Dutch to victory during the second conflict. His performance during the third Anglo-Dutch War saved the United Provinces from defeat. He was subsequently killed in action against the French. Painting by Ferdinand Bol (NMM BHC2997).

The real manpower crisis came in 1653, when many of these new ships entered service. The navy needed another 16,000 men to crew these vessels, and therefore was forced to enlist untrained 'landsmen' and boys, who would have to learn their craft the hard way, in the middle of a war. Another solution was to draft soldiers into the fleet, either as de facto marines, as gunners, or 'to perform as far as they are able all service as seamen'. Manning the fleet was even more of a problem after the Restoration, when a combination of corruption and the extravagance of the king meant that there was often little money left in the treasury to pay wages, or provide provisions for the navy.

The Dutch fleet had their own manning problems. Again, while the size of the fleet didn't vary very much, hired merchantmen were for the large part replaced by larger men-of-war, which meant that at the start of the Second Anglo-Dutch War the combined Dutch fleet needed to find approximately 17,000 new recruits. One of the main problems they encountered was the power and influence of the Dutch East India Company. Their sailors were paid more than those in the service of the provincial Admiralties, and consequently they had the pick of the available pool of seamen. Just as in England, press-gangs were used to help provide the sailors needed to man the ships, but the crew of Indiamen or the herring fleets were exempt from impressments, and so there never seemed enough seamen to go around. Unlike the English though, the Dutch had access to the ports of continental Europe, and so in time of war recruits were found in German or Scandinavian ports.

An idea of the manning requirements of the two fleets can be gleaned from the crew numbers of the following selection of warships that took part in the Four Days Battle, the major conflict of the Second Anglo-Dutch War.

Ship	Rate	Guns	Crew
Prince	1st	92	620
Royal Charles	1st	82	650
Royal James	1st	82	520
Royal Oak	2nd	76	450
Royal Katherine	2nd	76	450
Henry	2nd	72	440
Triumph	2nd	72	430
Vanguard	2nd	60	320
Fairfax	3rd	60	320
Gloucester	3rd	58	280
York	3rd	58	280
Yarmouth	4th	52	200
Assistance	4th	46	170
Providence	4th	34	140
Oxford	5th	26	100

Ship	Guns	Admiralty	Crew
Hollandia	80	Amsterdam	450
Gouden Leeuwen	50	Amsterdam	238
Asperen	34	Amsterdam	130
Eendracht	76	Maas	380
Klein Hollandia	54	Maas	230
Gorinchem	36	Maas	136
Westfriesland	78	Noorderkwartier	394
Wapen van Nassau	60	Noorderkwartier	250
Drie Helden Davids	48	Noorderkwartier	228
Groot Frisia	72	Friesland	392
Stad en Lande	52	Friesland	228
Klein Frisia	38	Friesland	177
Walcheren	70	Zeeland	380
Dordrecht	50	Zeeland	200
Zeeridder	36	Zeeland	158

From this it can be seen that for the most part English crews were allocated to warships in proportion to their rate and the number of guns they carried. Dutch manning levels were more haphazard, and while each provincial Admiralty had set quotas for each ship, these varied slightly, while still remaining in proportion to their English counterparts.

Ordnance

While the two fleets maintained an approximate parity of numbers during the three conflicts, the English enjoyed a distinct advantage in terms of firepower. Also, while the number of guns carried in these ships was roughly similar during the First Anglo-Dutch War, the English were more successful in adding more ordnance to their ships as the century progressed. Just as importantly, they also enjoyed superiority in term of gun size, and so even if two rival ships carried the same amount of ordnance, the English vessel tended to fire a heavier broadside than her Dutch counterpart.

This difference in firepower was the result of the weight limitations imposed on Dutch ships by their shallow coastal waters, and by the consistent English

An English iron 'culverin drake', or short 'culverin' or 18-pounder, bearing the coat of arms of the English Commonwealth on its barrel. This piece was recovered from the sea off Scheveningen, and is a rarity, as following the Restoration all Commonwealth emblems were removed from all ordnance that remained in service. The gun is now on display at Fort Nelson, outside Portsmouth (Trustees of the Royal Armouries).

A Dutch two-decker firing a broadside. The discharge of so many black powder weapons created dense clouds of white smoke that hung over the sea, and greatly reduced visibility during a sea fight. Painting by Willem van de Velde the Younger (Rijksmuseum, Amsterdam).

desire to emphasize firepower rather than the ability to manoeuvre. These seventeenth-century English warships were capable of firing a far larger size of broadside compared to similarly sized warships of the eighteenth century, which underlines the point about this being a deliberate policy of the period. After the three wars ended the balance between manoeuvrability and firepower swung the other way.

This English policy had its drawbacks. For a start it meant that English ships were slower and less agile than their Dutch counterparts. The weight and number of the ordnance carried meant that these English warships tended to ride lower in the water, which sometimes meant that the lower tier of gunports could sometimes not be opened in anything other than moderate weather conditions, for fear of the vessel capsizing. The advantage, of course, was that this allowed English designers to increase the weight of ordnance that could be carried. On Dutch ships the lower gun tier was approximately 30–50 centimetres higher above the waterline than on English ships – sufficient for the guns to be used in less favourable weather conditions.

An example of this policy of upgrading is the conversion of the 70-gun Dutch warship *Huis te Zwieten* in 1665. Her lower-deck armament of 18-pounders was removed, and replaced by 32-pounders. If a ship was found to be riding dangerously low in the water, then she would have her masts shortened, or have additional planking added at the waterline to improve stability – anything rather than reduce the size and weight of her armament.

One of the largest Dutch warships of the Second Anglo-Dutch War was the *Zeven Provincien* of the Maas Admiralty, the flagship of Admiral-General de Ruyter. She carried 80 guns – 12 36-pounders, 16 24-pounders, 14 18-pounders,

 THE BATTLE OF SCHEVENINGEN, 1653

The final naval clash of the First Anglo-Dutch War was the battle of Scheveningen (known as the battle of Ter Heijde in Holland), fought on 8–10 August 1653. The Commonwealth fleet under General-at-Sea Monck was blockading the Dutch coast, and with Dutch commerce at a standstill Admiral Tromp put to sea to break the blockade. After two days of skirmishing and manoeuvre battle proper was joined on the morning of 10 August. The Dutch had the weather gauge, and attacked, passing through the English line. The English retaliated by forming squadron-sized battle lines that sailed up and down past the huddle of Dutch ships, pouring shot into them. Tromp was killed by a sharpshooter during the early stages of the battle, but the loss of the Admiral was kept from the rest of the fleet until the battle was over.

To break up the English squadrons the initial Dutch attack was led by fireships. Although most of the English ships managed to avoid the threat, the 32-gun *Oak* was set on fire, and the 44-gun *Worcester* was badly damaged, but managed to put out the blaze. This scene shows the climax of the fireship attack, when the 60-gun English *Triumph* was attacked by two fireships, but deftly avoided them before almost colliding and being engulfed by a third blazing vessel. At the last minute the crew of the *Triumph* managed to fend off the blazing ship, but Rear-Admiral Graves, who directed the operation, was badly burned, and died of his wounds.

12 12-pounders and 26 6-pounders, giving her a broadside weight of 745 pounds. Just three other warships in the Dutch fleet carried these heavy 36-pounders, and only the *Westfriesland* of the Noorderkwartier Admiralty carried more than a pair of them; even then she only carried four. Even the *Hollandia*, the Amsterdam-built flagship of Vice-Admiral Cornelis Tromp carried nothing larger than ten 24-pounders, augmented by 18 18-pounders, 28 12-pounders and 24 5-pounders.

By contrast in 1666 the Duke of Albemarle's English flagship during the Four Days Battle was the *Royal Charles*, of 82 guns. She carried 20 42-pounders (cannon of seven), six 32-pounders (demi-cannon), 26 18-pounders (culverins) and 30 9-pounders (demi-culverins), firing a total broadside weight of 885 pounds, some 140 pounds more than the Dutch flagship. All English First and Second Rates carried either 42-pounders or 32-pounders, sometimes both. Similarly all but one of the Third Rates in the fleet, armed with 56–70 guns apiece, carried 32-pounders in their lowest gun deck. This is what gave the English ships their edge. The 80-gun *Hollandia* – one of the most powerfully armed warships in the Dutch fleet – fired a similar broadside weight to the smaller English Third Rates, such as the 60-gun *Fairfax*. If we look again at the warships we used as examples earlier, we can see just how significant this disparity in weight of firepower really was.

Ship	Rate	Guns	Weight of Broadside (in pounds)
Prince	1st	92	972
Royal Charles	1st	82	885
Royal James	1st	82	762
Royal Oak	2nd	76	769
Royal Katherine	2nd	76	777
Henry	2nd	72	666
Triumph	2nd	72	656
Vanguard	2nd	60	496
Fairfax	3rd	60	581
Gloucester	3rd	58	509
York	3rd	58	506
Yarmouth	4th	52	332
Assistance	4th	46	298
Providence	4th	34	154
Oxford	5th	26	119

Ship	Admiralty	Guns	Weight of Broadside (in pounds)
Hollandia	Amsterdam	80	568
Gouden Leeuwen	Amsterdam	50	276
Asperen	Amsterdam	34	135
Eendracht	Maas	76	586
Klein Hollandia	Maas	54	372
Gorinchem	Maas	36	162
Westfriesland	Noorderkwartier	78	556
Wapen van Nassau	Noorderkwartier	60	401
Drie Helden Davids	Noorderkwartier	48	260
Groot Frisia	Friesland	72	unknown
Stad en Lande	Friesland	52	302
Klein Frisia	Friesland	38	unknown
Walcheren	Zeeland	70	527
Dordrecht	Zeeland	50	276
Zeeridder	Zeeland	36	168

Given this difference in firepower it seems surprising that the Dutch were not simply blown out of the water. Instead they held their own against the English through a combination of superior seamanship, better leadership and strategic planning, innovative tactics, and a certain amount of luck.

Tactics

Before the First Anglo-Dutch War naval battles were little more than unplanned mêlées, resembling the aerial dogfights of the First World War rather than what we normally associate with naval battles of the age of sail.

This was less a result of poor discipline than choice. By allowing individual ship captains to manoeuvre as they liked during a battle, each ship and crew was able to take full advantage of its own capabilities. The Dutch in particular had witnessed the naval battles of the Spanish Armada, and concluded that firepower alone wasn't the arbiter of victory in naval combat. Therefore they developed a tactical doctrine based on a combination of fire and manoeuvre, seeking to overtake an opponent, then disable him by gunfire. Then they could either administer the *coup de grâce* by boarding the enemy vessel, or more likely force him to surrender by threatening to sink him by gunfire.

This tactical system that emphasized individuality had served the Dutch well at the battle of the Downs (1639), when they defeated a Spanish fleet. Dutch warship design was based on this doctrine, where small, nimble warships were preferred to large and less agile floating gun batteries. The

The battle of Scheveningen in 1653 was the hard-fought final engagement of the First Anglo-Dutch War. In this grisaille by Willem van de Velde the Elder the artist has included himself in the illustration, sketching the action from the deck of the small vessel in the foreground.

The opening engagement of the Second Anglo-Dutch War, the battle of Lowestoft, fought in June 1665, was a fiercely contested affair, but after the Dutch flagship *Eendracht* blew up the Dutch lost heart, and retired from the fight. In this sketch by Willem van de Velde the Elder the explosion can be seen in the middle right of the scene.

The battle of the Texel, fought in August 1673. In this painting by Willem van de Velde the Younger the fighting is shown concentrated around Prince Rupert's flagship HMS *Prince*, under attack from three Dutch warships (Felbrigg Hall, National Trust).

result was that at the start of the First Anglo-Dutch War in 1652, only the flagship of the fleet commander Admiral Tromp carried as many as 54 guns. The remainder carried fewer than 30 guns, but for the most part they were faster and more manoeuvrable than their English counterparts.

Across the North Sea the English felt that gunnery was the key, and so from 1610 on, when the *Prince Royal* was launched, the emphasis was on firepower rather than agility. During the English Civil War it was found that these powerful great ships were of little use against fast-sailing privateers, so frigates were built to counter this threat. However, rather than develop these as an adjunct to the main battle fleet, the English merely added more guns to them when the privateering threat had passed, effectively making them little more than smaller versions of the fleet's great ships. More importantly, the English failed to develop a tactical doctrine that would play to this strength in firepower.

As a result during the opening battles of the First Anglo-Dutch War the clashes developed into mêlées, which benefited the Dutch more than the

G   RAID ON THE MEDWAY, 1667

The foundations for the spectacular Dutch raid on the main English fleet anchorage in the River Medway were laid by Charles II. The extravagant expenditure of the King and his court had all but bankrupted the country, and so to save money the bulk of the fleet was placed in reserve during 1667. Instead the English relied on their coastal defences to keep the enemy at bay. The Medway was actually poorly defended, with just one fort at Sheerness guarding the mouth of the river, and a boom and a handful of gun batteries protecting the main anchorage further upstream. On 10 June the Dutch stormed and captured the fort at Sheerness, and the following day the fleet entered the river. On the morning of 12 June they broke the boom and negotiated the line of hastily sunk blockships. The English fleet was trapped and helpless, and the following day the Dutch arrived off Chatham, and burned or forced aground several major warships before departing for Holland, with the captured *Royal Charles* in tow. It was a humiliating blow for the Restoration navy, and it forced Charles II to sign an unfavourable peace treaty with the victors.

This plate shows the moment when the 36-gun Dutch warship *Vrede* from the Amsterdam Admiralty broke the boom. Beyond her lay the 42-gun Fourth Rate HMS *Unity* (formerly the *Eendracht*), which had been captured from the Dutch in 1665. The English warship was brushed aside, and forced to flee upriver to avoid the Dutch fireships that followed astern of the *Vrede*. She was captured the following day.

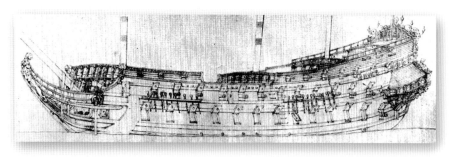

During the Second Anglo-Dutch War the sleek and fast two-decker *Hollandia* of 80 guns flew the flag of Lieutenant Admiral General Cornelis Tromp, the son of Admiral Maarten Tromp. Engraving by Willem van de Velde the Elder, 1666.

English. For their part the English had replaced their Civil War naval commanders with Generals-at-Sea – former land commanders who understood the need for firepower and formations, and who were suspicious of captains who used their initiative rather than following the wishes of their commanders. Of these Generals-at-Sea Richard Deane and Edward Popham were competent, but only Robert Blake displayed a true understanding of naval warfare, winning a string of victories that made him the most successful Admiral in British history, apart from Nelson. It was Deane – a gunnery expert – who finally produced the doctrine the English needed to win the war at sea.

His Instructions for the better *Ordering of the Fleet in Fighting* – or 'Fighting Instructions' of March 1653 were based on extensive consultations between him and Blake, and together they concocted a way of making the most of their advantage in firepower by ensuring that in battle 'all the ships of every squadron shall endeavour to keep in line with the chief'. In other words, the ships were expected to form into a line of battle. The guns of a sailing ship of war fired broadsides to each side. The bow and stern of a ship not only had virtually no guns mounted in them, save a few chase pieces, but these two ends of the vessel were vulnerable to enemy fire. A shot fired into them would pass right along the deck of a wooden-hulled warship, wreaking havoc as it went. At a stroke the *Fighting Instructions* not only avoided this problem by protecting the bow and stern of a warship, but it also made sure that as many guns as possible could fire on the enemy.

Admiral Tromp, commanding the Dutch fleet, realized the game was up. As long as the English fleet could maintain its formation, then the Dutch would be fighting at a disadvantage. He tried to break the English line at the battle of Scheveningen (1653) by using fireships, and while the tactic was successful up to a point, the English fleet was able to recover, reform, and then pound their way to victory. Tromp was killed in the process, and his successors were faced with finding a way to match the English tactic through forming a line of battle themselves, or by disrupting the English formation. Thereafter, Dutch tactics were a reaction to English ones – an attempt to even the odds by turning a battle back into one of manoeuvre rather than firepower.

When Popham died in 1651 he was replaced by George Monck, the only one of the leading Commonwealth commanders to remain in power after the Restoration. As Blake was in the Mediterranean it was Monck who led the English fleet to victory at Scheveningen. He was also responsible for bringing about the return of the monarchy. He proved a sound enough admiral, despite his tendency to use land commands at inopportune moments, such as ordering a squadron to 'wheel to the right' rather than to tack to starboard. During the Second Anglo-Dutch War he bolstered the less experienced royal commanders Prince Rupert and James, Duke of York (the future King James II and VII). This in turn gave York the experience he needed to command the fleet during the Third Anglo-Dutch conflict a few years later.

During this time both the English and the Dutch perfected their tactics and their command abilities, which were key to the successful prosecution of a naval battle during the age of sail. The Restoration navy developed a signalling system that remained in use in various forms until after the battle of Trafalgar a century and a half later. The Dutch also developed their own system, although each provincial admiralty followed its own guidelines, which in turn sometimes led to confusion. The real weakness of the Dutch fleet though, was its inability to successfully blend fire tactics with disruptive ones, and being unable to switch over to a mêlée battle when the opportunity arose.

The Zeeland admiralty in particular argued that only by instituting this kind of action, leading to close-range manoeuvre and boarding, would a decisive Dutch victory be achieved. Despite the extensive use of fireships, and attempts to isolate and overwhelm parts of the English fleet, the Dutch were largely unable to bring this about. Ship commanders were dismayed by the damage received by the few ships that came close enough to an English formation to breach the line of battle, and they were therefore unwilling to put themselves in harm's way. This conservative approach wasn't the answer, but even the States-General, the ruling body of the United Provinces, called for squadrons to operate together, in discrete formations, so reducing the risk of the isolation and loss of individual ships. The Dutch never developed an effective answer to the line of battle, and so they preferred to follow the safe middle course, of preventing their own destruction, rather than destroying the enemy. It would take another century and a half before Nelson found a way to break a line of battle, and to inflict a decisive defeat on the enemy. In the mid-seventeenth century both sides were still coming to terms with the tactical doctrines created during the three Anglo-Dutch wars, and learning the hard way just how effective these tactics could be.

THE SHIPS

Major warships of the English Fleet, 1652–74

| The early Stuart fleet | | | | | |
Name	Date Built	Rebuilt	Tonnage	Guns	Fate
Lion	1557	1583, 1609, 1658	626	38	Formerly *Golden Lion* (until 1609) and *Red Lion* (until 1640). Sold 1698
Vanguard	1586	1599, 1615, 1631	750	40–56	Scuttled 1667
Rainbow		1602, 1617	650	40–56	Sunk as breakwater (Sheerness) 1680
Resolution	1610	1641, 1663	1,187	70–80	Formerly *Prince Royal*. Renamed *Royal Prince* 1660. Burned by Dutch 1666
Entrance	1619	-	404	30	Formerly *Happy Entrance*. Burned 1658
Garland	1620	-	420	34–40	Captured by Dutch, 1652
Victory		1666	870	42–56	Broken up 1691
Bonadventure	1621	-	410	32	Lost in action 1653
Swiftsure		1653	876	42	Captured by Dutch 1666.
George	1622	-	895	42–56	Formerly *St. George* (until 1648). Hulked 1687
Andrew		-	895	42–56	Formerly *St. Andrew* (until 1648). Wrecked 1666
Triumph	1623	-	921	42–64	Broken up 1687
Paragon	1633	-	793	42	Formerly *Henrietta Maria*. Burned at sea 1655
James	1634	-	875	48–60	Renamed *Old James* 1660. Sold 1682
Unicorn		-	823	46–56	Sold 1687
Leopard	1635	-	515	34	Captured by Dutch 1653
Sovereign	1637	1660 and post-war	1,522	90–100	Formerly *Sovereign of the Seas*. Renamed *Royal Sovereign* 1660. Burned 1697

Note: the names and displacement given here are those used during the First Anglo-Dutch War (1652–54). Where two numbers are given for the number of guns carried, the first is earlier in the ship's career (i.e. during the First Anglo-Dutch War, and the second is her post-Restoration armament.

Name	Date Built	Rebuilt	Tonnage	Guns	Fate
Parliamentarian and Commonwealth additions					
Constant Warwick	1645	1666	342	32	Privateer, purchased 1649. Captured by French 1691
Assurance	1646	-	340	32–40	Sold 1698
Adventure		-	385	34–40	Captured by French 1709
Nonsuch		-	394	34	Wrecked 1664
Dragon	1647	Post-war	470	38–46	Wrecked 1711
Elizabeth		-	474	38	Burned by Dutch 1667
Phoenix		-	414	38	Briefly captured by Dutch 1652. Wrecked 1664
Tiger		Post-war	453	38–40	Wrecked 1743
Fairfax	1650	-	743	52	Burned 1653
Speaker		Post-war	727	50–62	Renamed *Mary* 1660. Wrecked 1703
Portsmouth		-	422	38–46	Captured by French and blown up 1689
President		1666 and post-war	462	38–48	Renamed *Bonadventure* 1660. Broken up 1711
Reserve		Post-war	513	40–48	Foundered 1703
Advice		Post-war	516	40–48	Captured by the French 1711
Pelican		-	500	36	Burned 1656
Centurion		-	531	40–48	Wrecked 1689
Foresight		-	522	40–48	Wrecked 1698
Assistance		Post-war	522	40–48	Sunk as breakwater 1746
Antelope	1651	-	828	56	Wrecked 1652
Worcester		Post-war	662	48–60	Renamed *Dunkirk* 1660. Broken up 1749
Sapphire		-	442	38–46	Wrecked 1671
Laurel		-	489	48	Wrecked 1657
Ruby		-	556	40–48	Captured by French 1707
Diamond		-	550	40–48	Captured by French 1693
Kentish	1652	-	550	40–48	Renamed *Kent* 1660. Wrecked 1672
Sussex		-	601	40–48	Blew up 1653
Fairfax (II)	1653	-	756	52	Wrecked 1682
Plymouth		Post-war	742	52–60	Foundered 1705
Essex		-	652	48	Captured by Dutch 1666
Hampshire		Post-war	479	38–46	Lost in action 1697
Portland		-	605	40–48	Burned 1692
Newcastle		Post-war	631	44–54	Wrecked 1703
Bristol		Post-war	532	44–48	Captured by French, then recaptured and sunk 1707
Yarmouth		-	608	44–54	Broken up 1680
Gloucester	1654	-	755	50–60	Wrecked 1682
Torrington		-	732	52–62	Renamed *Dreadnought* 1660. Foundered 1690
Newbury		-	766	52–62	Renamed *Revenge* 1660. Condemned 1678
Bridgewater		-	743	52	Renamed *Anne* 1660. Blew up 1673
Lyme		Post-war	764	52–62	Renamed *Montague* 1660. Broken up 1749
Marston Moor		-	734	52–60	Renamed *York* 1660. Wrecked 1703
Langport		-	781	50–62	Renamed *Henrietta* 1660. Wrecked 1689
Tredagh		-	885	50–60	Also known as *Drogheda*. Renamed *Resolution* 1660. Burned 1666
London		-	1,104	64	Blew up 1665
Taunton		Post-war	536	40–48	Renamed *Crowne* 1660. Wrecked 1719
Dover		Post-war	554	40–48	Broken up 1730
Winsby		-	605	44–54	Renamed *Happy Return* 1660. Captured by French 1691
Naseby	1655	-	1,258	80	Renamed *Royal Charles* 1661. Captured by the Dutch 1667
Dunbar	1656	-	1,082	64–82	Renamed *Henry* 1660. Burned 1682
Richard	1658	-	1,108	70	Renamed *Royal James* 1660. Burned by Dutch 1667
Monck	1659	Post-war	703	52–60	Wrecked 1720

Early Restoration additions					
Name	Date Built	Rebuilt	Tonnage	Guns	Fate
Royal Oak	1664	-	1,021	76	Burned by the Dutch 1667
Royal Katherine		Post-war	1,108	84–86	Renamed Ramillies 1709. Wrecked 1760
Loyal London	1666	-	1,236	80	Burned 1667
Cambridge		-	881	70	Wrecked 1694
Rupert		Post-war	791	66–64	Broken up 1740
Defiance		-	863	64	Burned 1668
Warspite		Post-war	885	70–68	Renamed Edinburgh 1721. Broken up 1771
Greenwich		Post-war	646	54–60	Wrecked 1744
St. Patrick		-	670	50	Captured by Dutch 1667
St. David	1667	-	685	54	Foundered 1690
Monmouth		Post-war	856	66	Broken up 1767

Mid-Restoration additions					
Name	Date Built	Rebuilt	Tonnage	Guns	Fate
Resolution	1667	Post-war	885	70–68	Foundered 1703
Charles	1668	Post-war	1,229	96	Renamed St. George 1701. Broken up 1774
Edgar		Post-war	994	72–74	Burned 1711
St. Michael	1669	Post-war	1,101	90–96	Renamed Marlborough 1706. Foundered 1762
Prince	1670	Post-war	1,403	100	Renamed Royal William 1692. Broken up 1813
London		Post-war	1,328	96	Broken up 1747
St. Andrew		Post-war	1,338	96	Renamed Royal Anne 1703. Broken up 1727
Royal James	1671	-	1,416	100	Lost in action 1672
Royal Charles	1673	Post-war	1,443	100	Renamed Queen 1693, Royal George 1715, Royal Anne 1756. Broken up 1767.

Later Restoration additions					
Name	Date Built	Rebuilt	Tonnage	Guns	Fate
Swiftsure	1673	Post-war	978	70	Renamed Revenge 1716. Sold 1787
Harwich	1674	-	993	70–64	Wrecked 1691
Royal Oak		Post-war	1,107	74	Broken up 1764
Oxford		Post-war	677	54	Broken up 1758
Defiance	1675	Post-war	890	64	Broken up 1749
Kingfisher		Post-war	663	46	Broken up 1728
Woolwich		Post-war	761	54	Broken up 1747

Major warships of the Dutch Fleet, 1665–67

The information covering the Dutch fleet is far more fragmentary. Therefore, this list is presented in a different way. It contains the Dutch warships active during the Second Anglo-Dutch War, divided by regional admiralty.

Note that some ship names are used several times by different provincial admiralties, and even within the same provincial fleet.

Friesland Admiralty

Name	Guns	In Service	Note
Groot Frisia	72	1665–92	
Groningen	72	1668–88	
Prins Hendrik Casimir	72	1665–92	
Ooostergo	60	1653–76	
Westergo	56	1653–72	Lost in action 1672
Elf Steden	54	1654–74	
Stad en Lande	52	1653–76	
Prinses Albertina	50	1658–67	
Omlandia	48	1654–88	
Klein Frisia	38	1653–76	
Zevenwolden	58	1664–66	Captured by English 1666, then recaptured
Rie van Sneek	66	1665–66	Lost in action 1666
Groningen (II)	44	1658–65	Captured by English 1665
Postillon van Smirna	40	1665–66	Hired
Hollandia	40	1665–66	Hired

Zeeland Admiralty

Name	Guns	In Service	Notes
Walcheren	70	1666–89	Wrecked 1689
Tholen	60	1665–66	Lost in action 1666
Zieriksee	60	1653–74	Purchased from VOC
Hof van Zeeland	58	1665–66	Lost in action 1666
Utrecht	50	1653–73	Purchased from VOC
Middleburg	50	1653–93	
Vlissingen	50	1653–74	Purchased from VOC
Kampveere	50	1653–73	Captured by English 1673
Dordrecht	50	1653–73	
Wapen van Zeeland	36	1665–67	
Delft	36	1665–74	Frigate
Zeelandia	36	1666–68	Frigate
Zeeridder	34	1653–67	Frigate
Schakerlo	30	-	Frigate
Goes	30	1652–88	Frigate
Zwanenburg	30	1655	Frigate. Lost in action 1665

BELOW LEFT

This view of the 42–50 gun Dutch warship *Gouda*, built by the Amsterdam Admiralty in 1656, provides a clear view of her stern transom, decorated with a depiction of the town of Gouda, on the River Ijsel. Engraving by Willem van de Velde the Younger, c.1664.

BELOW RIGHT

One of seven Dutch warships of the period to bear the same name, the *Zeelandia* of 58 guns was built in 1653, and was burned in action during the battle of Lowestoft (1665). She flies the ensign of the Zeeland Admiralty at her stern, rather than the usual tricolour of the United Provinces. Sketch by Willem van de Velde the Elder.

Amsterdam Admiralty Name	Guns	In Service	Notes
Hollandia	80	1665–83	Wrecked 1683
Gouda	72	1656–83	Wrecked 1683
Reiger(sbergen)	72	1665–90	
Calantsoog	70	1664–89	aka Kalantsoog
Liefde	70	1661–66	Lost in action 1666
Amsterdam	68	1653–89	Captured by French 1689
Oosterwijk	68	1653–76	
Geloof	68	1661–74	
Spiegel	68	1663–76	
Wapen van Utrecht	66	-	
Deventer	66	1665–73	Wrecked 1673
Provincie Utrecht	64	1663–96	
Huis te Kruiningen	60	1653–77	Lost in action 1677
Stad en Lande	60	1653–71	
Huis Tijdverdijf	58	1655–83	Wrecked 1683
Hilversum	58	1655–67	Captured by English 1667
Luipaard	58	1653–65	English prize (Leopard), 1653
Vrijheid	56	1651–76	Lost in action 1676
Koevorden	56	1665–66	Lost in action 1665
Gelderland	56	1656–69	Originally of 44 guns
Beschermer	54	1666–77	Captured by French 1677
Gouden Leeuw	52	1666–83	Wrecked 1683
Zuiderhuis	50	1653–76	
Landman	48	1653–66	Lost in action 1666
Vrede	48	1650–67	
Stad Gouda	48	1656–83	Wrecked 1683
Dom van Utrecht	48	1654–88	
Stavoren	48	1653–72	Captured by English 1672
Wakende Boei	48	1661–76	
Doesburg	48	1665–77	Sold to Denmark
Vereenigte Provincien	48	1665–67	Hired from VOC
Duivenvoorde	48	1661–76	
Tromp	48	1655–67	
Huis te Jaarsveld	48	1653–76	
Raadhuis van Haarlem	48	1658–67	Captured by English 1667
Groningen	48	1641–67	Sold to Denmark
Zon	48	-	
Kampen	48	1640–66	
Vrede	46	1650–67	
(Ter) Goes	46	1641–65	Lost in action 1665
Harderwijk	46	1662–93	
Haarlem	46	1644–66	
Zeelandia	38	1643–77	Lost in action 1677
Harderin	38	1641–65	Lost in action 1665
Maagd van Enkhuizen	38	1651–65	Purchased from VOC
Phesant	38	1653–65	
(Wappen van) Edam	38	1644–65	Captured by English 1665, then recaptured and lost action, also 1665
Schager Roos	38	1665	
Ijlst	36	1653–65	Frigate
Overijssel	36	1650–86	Frigate
Asperen	36	1656–89	Frigate
Harder	34	1658–66	Frigate. Lost in action 1666
Vollenhoven	30	1665	Frigate

Maas Admiralty			
Name	Guns	In Service	Notes
Zeven Provincien	80	1665–94	
Eendracht	76	1653–65	Lost in action 1665
Groot Hollandia	68	1654–87	
Ridderschap	66	1666–90	Foundered 1690
Gelderland	66	1666–95	
Delft	62	1666–89	
Klein Hollandia	58	1656–72	Lost in action
Wassenaar	58	1666–81	Wrecked 1681
Wapen van Utrecht	56	1666–71	Wrecked 1671
Prins Mauritus	54	1653–65	aka Prins Mauritius. Lost in action 1665
Stadt Utrecht	48	1653–65	
Dordrecht	46	1666–86	
Rotterdam	46	1658–65	
Vrede	40	1665	
Prinses Louise	40	1646–74	
Delft (II)	36	1658–65	Captured by English 1665
Gorinchem	36	1639–71	Expended as fireship 1671
Wapen van Utrecht (II)	36	1661–86	
Nijmegen	34	1666–67	
Harderwijk	32	1659–88	

With nearly 200 ships involved, the Four Days Battle (1–4 June 1666) has been described as the largest sea fight of the age of sail. In this depiction of the battle the composition is dominated by the *Zeven Provincien* and the *Royal Prince*. In the foreground the crew of the battered and barely floating *Swiftsure* surrender to a Dutch boarding party. Painting by Abraham Storck (NMM BHC0286).

ABOVE LEFT
The largest ship in the Dutch fleet during the First Anglo-Dutch War, the *Brederode* of 56 guns served as the flagship of Admiral Maarten Tromp. She was up-gunned slightly after the war, but was sunk in 1658, while in action against the Swedes. Engraving by Willem van de Velde the Elder.

ABOVE RIGHT
The simple, elegant lines of the small 24-gun Dutch warship *Postillon* (also *Postiljon*) of the Amsterdam Admiralty. During the third Anglo-Dutch War she served as a commerce raider and an escort vessel. Engraving by Willem van de Velde the Younger.

Noorderkwartier			
Name	Guns	In Service	Notes
Westfriesland	78	1666–83	
Pacificatie	74	1665–86	
Maagd van Enkhuizen	72	-	
Jonge Prins	66	1666–86	
Gelderland	64	1654–86	
Noorderkwartier	60	1664–86	
Wapen van Nassau	60	1664–86	
Hollandse Tuin	56	1664–65	
Jozua	54	1655–72	Lost in action 1672
Drei Helden Davids	50	1654–86	
Caleb	50	1658–74	
Wapen van Holland	48	-	
Wapen van Medemblik	46	-	
Jupiter	44	1653–86	
Eendracht	44	1639–76	Lost in action 1676
Prinses Roijaal	40	1641–65	
Eenhorn	30	-	
Hoorn	30	1665	
Wapen van Hoorn	30	1665	Frigate
Kastel van Medemblik	30	1640–66	Frigate

The steeply sloping quarterdeck of the Dutch warship *Huis te Jaarsveld* of 48 guns, built by the Amsterdam Admiralty in 1653. She was a partial three-decker, as her upper gundeck was split by her lofty sterncastle. Engraving by Willem van de Velde the Elder.

Dutch East Indiamen			
Name	Guns	In Service	Fate
Maarsveveen	78	All 1665 only	Lost in action 1665
Oranje	76		Lost in action 1665
Delfland	70		
Huis te Zweiten	70		Captured by English 1665
Carolus Quintus	54		Rehired in 1667, and lost in action
Nagelboom	52		Captured by English 1665, recaptured 1667
Beurs van Amsterdam	52		
Niuw Batavia	50		
Mars	50		Captured by English 1665
Sphera Mundi	41		
Agatha	32		Sold to Denmark 1666

FURTHER READING

A number of excellent books are available in English, covering various aspects of the ships, fleets and battles of this tumultuous period. This is less a detailed bibliography than a list of suggested titles, for those who want to delve a little deeper into the subject.

Barratt, John, *Cromwell's Wars at Sea*, Pen & Sword, Barnsley (2006)

Blok, P., *The Life of Admiral de Ruyter*, Greenwood, London (1985), translation of 1933 edition

Capp, Bernard, *Cromwell's Navy*, OUP, Oxford (1988)

Cordingly, David (ed.), *The Art of the Van de Veldes*, National Maritime Museum, Greenwich (1989)

Corbett, Julian, '*Fighting Instructions, 1530–1816*', Naval Records Society, London (1905)

Fox, Frank, *Great Ships: The Battlefleet of King Charles II*, Conway Maritime Press, London (1980)

Fox, Frank L., *The Four Days' Battle of 1666: The Greatest Sea Fight of the Age of Sail*, Seaforth Publishing, Barnsley (2009)

Gardiner, Robert (ed.), *The Line of Battle: The Sailing Warship, 1650–1840*, Conway Maritime Press (Conway's History of the Ship Series), London (1992)

Hainsworth, Roger and Churches, Christine, *The Anglo-Dutch Naval Wars, 1652–74*, Sutton Publishing, Stroud (1998)

Howarth, David, *The Men-of-War*, Time Life Books (Seafarers Series), Amsterdam (1978)

Lavery, Brian, *The Ship of the Line*, Conway Maritime Press, London (1983)

Oppenheim, M., *A History of the Administration of the Royal Navy, 1509–1660*, Temple Smith, London (1988)

Tedder, Arthur W., *The Navy of the Restoration*, OUP, Oxford (2010)

Vreugdenhil, A., *Ships of the United Netherlands, 1648–1702*, Naval Records Society, London (1938)

TOP
HMS *Royal Sovereign* as she looked after her refit in 1660. During this refurbishment her forecastle and sterncastle were lowered, and much of her remaining decoration was removed. Engraving by Willem van de Velde the Elder (Royal Canterbury Museum).

BELOW
The *Portland* was a Fourth Rate frigate of the Ruby class, launched in 1653. She was one of 13 large frigates of her class, which were in turn slightly smaller versions of the earlier Speaker class, and improvements on the earlier 13 frigates of the Elizabeth class. Engraving by Willem van de Velde the Elder.

INDEX

Note: numbers in **bold** refer to illustrations and plates